D0016635

George Heslop

JOHN BECK   DEREK HAYLES

Footballers' HAIRCUTS

Text by Cris Freddi

WEIDENFELD & NICOLSON

Foreword by Chris Waddle

When I got asked to write the foreword for the book I must admit I did laugh. Footballers' haircuts have always been a talking point: on the terraces, in the dressing room and on TV. It's only a surprise that there hasn't been a book on them before now. And within these pages you are in for some real treats.

I feel it is only fair to tell you a true story behind one of my own more famous hairstyles. When I signed for Newcastle I began to grow my hair long. But I always had the problem where it frizzed out at the back. I got really frustrated, and so I ended up arranging to see my wife's cousin who was a hairdresser. She told me the best thing to do would be to get a loose perm. She said it would make my hair straighter. So I did it. I was playing for the first team now and one night after training I had it done. It was meant to be loose but instead it was really tight. So I had my hair flowing over my ears, flat on top, with a side parting and a perm at the back. It looked terrible.

I went to training next day and got hammered by the lads. By the Saturday it was no better. In those days we didn't really go out for a pre-match warm up, so when I ran out at 2.55pm it was the first time the crowd had seen it.

Usually, when you ran out at St. James's the fans would cheer at you and then sing your name. This time as I ran out on to the pitch all I heard was an 'oooh' from the whole crowd. The first time I got the ball for a throw-in the fans were all shouting at me, 'What have you done to your hair?'

The strangest part of it was, two weeks later I ran out and there must have been 10,000 people with my haircut! They had special offers around town – ten quid for the Waddle perm!

So a bit like Beckham, wherever I have played the people in the area, especially the kids, have copied my haircuts. It was the same when I was in France. For some reason though, I was never looked upon as a fashion icon. I must have been ahead of my time.

Paul Cant

Contents

ALDERSHOT FC

MIKE McGIVEN

BRIAN LITTLE

Introduction

We need our footballers to have hair.

That or no hair at all. It's what makes them recognisable on the pitch. Those names on the backs of their shirts, they only work on TV – so we need Paul Scholes' ginger nut, Carlos Valderramma's yellow fright wig or Frank Leboeuf's judicious use of the razor. Anything that helps them stand out.

It matters to them, too. Tom Priestly, who won two caps for Ireland in 1930, played in a rugby scrum-cap to hide his baldness. Guus Dräger wore a hairnet when he played for Holland against England in 1946. Bobby Mikhailov, who kept goal for Bulgaria in the 1994 World Cup, had a hair transplant and owned a wig-making firm.

This book is a tribute to that kind of, let's say, self-awareness. A celebration of the lengths footballers have gone to over the years. To justify its inclusion in these pages, a photo has to answer only one question: does it have the power to amaze? Whether they followed a fashion or set a trend (especially a trend others didn't have the nerve to follow), the hairstyles within these pages are certainly amazing.

Billy Seddon

1890s	1890	1891	1892	1893	1894	1895	1896	1897	1898	1899
1900s	1900	1901	1902	1903	1904	1905	1906	1907	1908	1909
1910s	1910	1911	1912	1913	1914	1915	1916	1917	1918	1919
1920s	1920	1921	1922	1923	1924	1925	1926	1927	1928	1929
1930s	1930	1931	1932	1933	1934	1935	1936	1937	1938	1939
1940s	1940	1941	1942	1943	1944	1945	1946	1947	1948	1949
1950s	1950	1951	1952	1953	1954	1955	1956	1957	1958	1959

1890–1959

Let's Keep this Short

We'll start with a chapter on early footballers' haircuts – and there's no point letting it grow too long. We just haven't got the raw material.

The bottom line is this. In all the years before 1960, hairstyles didn't change all that much. You won't find a single footballer with hair that covered his ears, and as for anything long enough to touch the collar, that would have been positively unnatural.

When common decency obliges you to have a short back and sides, all you can do is tinker with the top. Grease it back or crew-cut it, add the odd centre parting or grand Victorian moustache – that's about it. And wish you were born forty years later.

RALPH SQUIRE

ROBERT BRUCE

BOB BARCLAY

Eric Houghton

1932 Don't be fooled. Under that Nigel Kennedy haircut lay one of the hardest shots in the game. Get in the way of Eric Houghton's left foot and you never played the violin again. When he scored from a deflected free kick in a famous win over Austria in 1932, it's said that the defender was still rubbing his head ten minutes later. A goalscoring winger, Eric hit five in his seven games for England, plus 160 for Aston Villa in the League, and was the club's manager the last time they won the FA Cup, back in 1957.

THAULOW GOBERG

PAUL JANES

1934 This particular 'Herr cut' is typical of the Thirties. Paul Janes was certainly a man of his age, right down to the Nazi salute he gave before the match with England at White Hart Lane. He played 71 times for Germany, won the league title with Fortuna Düsseldorf, and was such a cool full-back he didn't always need to undo the strings of his shirt.

England 1955

1955 We find Captain Billy a bit quaint nowadays. That ice cream quiff, the big shorts, the 'making rugs at home, embroidering tablecloths or table-runners' he listed as hobbies. And he led England to some of their most famous defeats: USA 1950, Hungary 1953 and 1954. But he was also the first footballer to win 100 caps, he won the FA Cup and three League titles with Wolves, and check out those thighs: this was a central defender you didn't mess with. His marriage to one of the singing Beverley Sisters made them the Posh 'n' Becks of their day. Sort of.

Mr & Mrs Jimmy Greaves

BOBBY ROBSON

1958 Three of today's best-loved personalities in their youthful pomp, sharing the clean-cut look that was fashionable at the end of the Fifties. Jimmy Greaves has just got married at eighteen (another sign of the times) and is already on his way to a record 357 goals in the top flight, another 44 for England, and the love of rival fans from Chelsea and Tottenham.

We know all about Sir Bobby Robson's success as a manager, but he could play a bit as well, scoring two goals on his England debut and another two in the 9-3 thrashing of Scotland in 1961. And he'll still tell you all about the two that were disallowed in the 1958 World Cup.

Bobby Charlton

1959

Here's someone waiting for long hair to come along and soften his features. Yes, this is *the* Ally MacLeod, Scotland's manager in their disastrous 1978 World Cup bid. The action shot shows him heading the winner for Third Lanark against Rangers, and the crew-cut belongs to his time at Blackburn Rovers, when he played in the 1960 FA Cup Final. That prominent hooter was always his trademark. When he became Scotland boss, he told us 'Concorde has landed.' Oh, and 'My name is Ally MacLeod and I am a winner.'

ALLY MACLEOD

Bobby Charlton

1960	JAN	FEB	MAR	APL	MAY	JUN	JUL	AUG	SEP	OCT	NOV	DEC
1961	JAN	FEB	MAR	APL	MAY	JUN	JUL	AUG	SEP	OCT	NOV	DEC
1962	JAN	FEB	MAR	APL	MAY	JUN	JUL	AUG	SEP	OCT	NOV	DEC
1963	JAN	FEB	MAR	APL	MAY	JUN	JUL	AUG	SEP	OCT	NOV	DEC
1964	JAN	FEB	MAR	APL	MAY	JUN	JUL	AUG	SEP	OCT	NOV	DEC
1965	JAN	FEB	MAR	APL	MAY	JUN	JUL	AUG	SEP	OCT	NOV	DEC
1966	JAN	FEB	MAR	APL	MAY	JUN	JUL	AUG	SEP	OCT	NOV	DEC
1967	JAN	FEB	MAR	APL	MAY	JUN	JUL	AUG	SEP	OCT	NOV	DEC
1968	JAN	FEB	MAR	APL	MAY	JUN	JUL	AUG	SEP	OCT	NOV	DEC
1969	JAN	FEB	MAR	APL	MAY	JUN	JUL	AUG	SEP	OCT	NOV	DEC

1960–1969

Beyond the Fringe

They're remembered as the Swinging Sixties – but although they may have swung in certain sections of society, most of the country was still emerging from the post-war period. So don't expect any bouffant hairstyles or anything of hippy length. Apart from George Best's, there weren't even many Beatle's haircuts – and Bobby Charlton's comb-over was probably just as typical of the decade. We've found some individual gems – but it was essentially a kind of transit lounge between the short cuts of the Fifties and the explosion of the Seventies.

RON ATKINSON

1962 This is Big Ron early doors, already covering across in defence, moving his hair from one side of the area to the other. People chuckle about his playing ability too – but Oxford United remember him with affection. He joined them when they were still a non-League club and helped them to assorted promotions and the old Third Division title in 1968. If his career as a manager and commentator are anything to go by, you suspect he didn't always keep his thoughts to himself on the pitch.

Martin Peters

1966 In some ways this is the weirdest haircut of the lot. In a decade that treated footballers like pop stars, Martin Peters wore his hair like a schoolboy or an office manager – and wore it like that throughout a long career. Like the man himself, it didn't exactly stand out – although he was clever at ghosting in to score from midfield, fans didn't always appreciate his value. His goal in the 1966 World Cup Final sums it up: it would have been the winner if West Germany hadn't equalised in the last minute. Instead his West Ham team mate Geoff Hurst (who also kept the same hairstyle for years) got the knighthood.

BOBBY CHARLTON

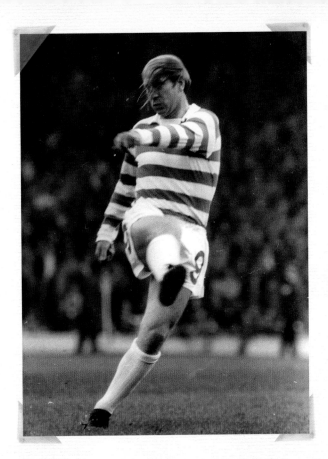

1968

Bobby Charlton was famous for two things: fearsome shooting power, and a comb-over hairstyle that refused to stick to its position on the pitch. Still, it didn't stop him scoring a record 49 goals for England, and it moved aside when he headed one of his two goals that won the 1968 European Cup Final for Man United ('It skidded off my bald patch'). The comb-over's long gone, but not the memory of those long-range cannonballs.

GEORGE BEST

1969 George and Sir Bobby made that United team famous, but they couldn't have been more different. From the early fringe that made him 'the fifth Beatle' to the Seventies sideburns and flowing locks, George had the game's highest profile on and off the pitch. Being the first footballing sex symbol brought the kind of problems we'd all like to have – but it did cut his career far too short. He was the type of player that makes you glad television was around.

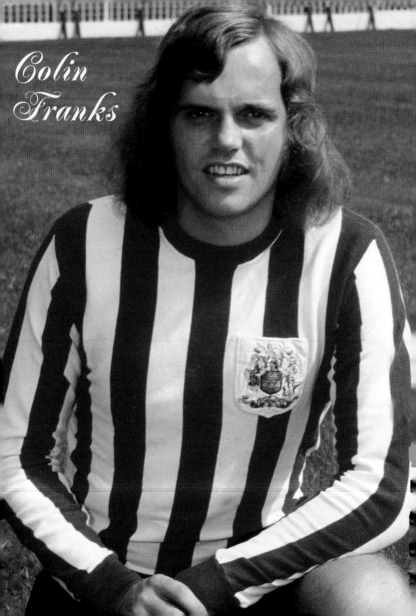

Colin
Franks

1970	JAN	FEB	MAR	APL	MAY	JUN	JUL	AUG	SEP	OCT	NOV	DEC
1971	JAN	FEB	MAR	APL	MAY	JUN	JUL	AUG	SEP	OCT	NOV	DEC
1972	JAN	FEB	MAR	APL	MAY	JUN	JUL	AUG	SEP	OCT	NOV	DEC
1973	JAN	FEB	MAR	APL	MAY	JUN	JUL	AUG	SEP	OCT	NOV	DEC
1974	JAN	FEB	MAR	APL	MAY	JUN	JUL	AUG	SEP	OCT	NOV	DEC
1975	JAN	FEB	MAR	APL	MAY	JUN	JUL	AUG	SEP	OCT	NOV	DEC
1976	JAN	FEB	MAR	APL	MAY	JUN	JUL	AUG	SEP	OCT	NOV	DEC
1977	JAN	FEB	MAR	APL	MAY	JUN	JUL	AUG	SEP	OCT	NOV	DEC
1978	JAN	FEB	MAR	APL	MAY	JUN	JUL	AUG	SEP	OCT	NOV	DEC
1979	JAN	FEB	MAR	APL	MAY	JUN	JUL	AUG	SEP	OCT	NOV	DEC

1970–1979

The Lengths They Went To

Right. This is where it all kicks off. The decade that fashion forgot? Well, perhaps. But it was also a time when men remembered it was physically possible to grow their hair below the base of their skulls. We'd been living in the 19th century for long enough.

Influences ranged from flower power to black power to glam-rock and disco. After that it was just a matter of multiplication. Grow your hair longer and any differences will show up a lot more. Straight hair looks straighter, curly hair erupts into an overgrown Brillo pad, everything just becomes more visible. After the restrictive practices of the previous hundred years, men were suddenly free to make their own mistakes.

1971

Big Pat Jennings illustrates the approach taken by too many men of his era. Keep your old haircut, just grow it longer. So this is essentially a Martin Peters untailored to a Seventies length, with Engelbert Humperdinck sideburns attached. It didn't stop your man from being arguably the greatest goalkeeper of all time. Completely self-taught, with hands like hams, he won the FA Cup with Tottenham and Arsenal and played the last of his 119 matches for Northern Ireland, a world record at the time, in the 1986 World Cup. It was his 41st birthday, but he still hadn't treated himself to a new hairstyle.

PAT JENNINGS

Neil Warnock

KEVIN BEATTIE

1972 Nice try Kevin, but even a Late-Renaissance study like this can't make a rottweiler angelic. At eighteen, big Kevin was already a fixture in Bobby Robson's Ipswich Town defence. He headed a goal for England against Scotland and might have won 100 caps if he hadn't been so injury prone. Cartilage problems, boiling chip pans that spilled over him, encounters with dodgy hairdressers – they all made sure we never saw the best of him.

Hard to know which is scarier. Neil Warnock as your manager when you've played badly and lost. Or Neil Warnock's wraparound hairstyle from his days as a winger in the lower divisions. We'll leave you to tell him.

1973 You'd think the lank locks would get in the way when he played, but they didn't stop cheeky Charlie from thumping the winner in the 1971 FA Cup Final. Long-bodied and full of flair, he won the Double with Arsenal and hit a hat-trick for Derby County against Real Madrid. But he played only 65 minutes for England, by which time he'd switched to the kind of perm we didn't have the heart to put on display.

Charlie George

1975 The blond Viking look added glamour to the middle of the park. The smile suggests Tony Currie believed it too. His skills took Sheffield United to the top of the League for a while and he pulled some stylish strings at Leeds. But three successive England managers weren't so sure, and his 17 caps were spread over seven years (and about forty visits to the hairdressers).

TONY CURRIE

STEVE BRUCE

Hard to believe this choirboy would one day grow into the hard-nosed central defender who captained Man United to their first League title in 26 years and the manager who brought Birmingham City back into the Premiership. This is the Steve Bruce of 1979 vintage, on his way to playing 200 League games for Gillingham. If he tells you the haircut was fashionable at the time, it's safer to believe him.

Ralph Coates

1976 Ralphie Coates was Bobby Charlton's heir apparent. Well you can tell that by looking at him. But we mean as a player too: he was almost as talented. In the end it didn't happen – but they did share the same stage for a moment. Ralph's first match for England was Sir Bobby's 100th. No wonder Northern Ireland lost: they were seeing double.

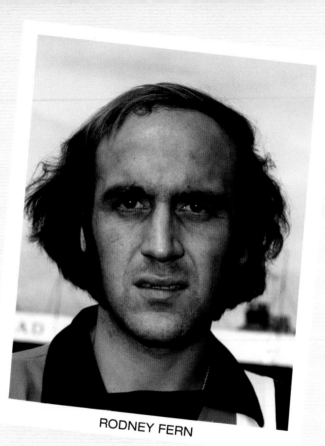

RODNEY FERN

1976 Behold a classic Seventies solution to thinning hair: prove you can grow it elsewhere. Rodney Fern played in an FA Cup Final for Leicester City when he was twenty, and scored a goal every three games for Chesterfield and Rotherham. A worrying sight for any defender.

Oh no. No, no, no, no, no. Graham seems to have changed his name to French because his real surname (Lafite) was exactly that. Unfortunately he adapted his hairstyle as well. This is what happens when you grow it like everybody else but haven't got the hair for it. He grew up with a short Sixties cut but played for Luton into the Seventies, and this was the result. Sometimes you should just say no. Or *non*.

GRAHAM FRENCH

TREVOR FRANCIS
BIRMINGHAM CITY AFC

1977 This is what League managers look like before they grow up. Trevor 'Superboy' Francis was only sixteen when he scored four goals in a game for Birmingham City. Nottingham Forest made him Britain's first million-pound player, and he repaid them by heading the only goal of a European Cup Final. Don't let the boyish looks distract you. Even as a young man he was a match for Brian Clough in transfer negotiations, and as a manager he's been known to administer the odd clip round the ear – a trick he might have picked up from the master.

GEORGE BERRY

1978 Talk about cushioned headers. If you're going to grow an Afro, grow a real Afro. George Berry had the biggest in British football. It turned him into six foot three of serious central defender. The first black player since 1931 to be capped by Wales, he was born in West Germany, who gave him a tough time in Euro 1980, winning 2-0 on his debut and 5-1 in Cologne. He did better at club level, winning the League Cup with Wolves and using his communication skills ('a bit wearing on the eardrums') as captain of Stoke City.

GERRY FRANCIS & MIKE FLANAGAN
CRYSTAL PALACE

1979 Gerry Francis' career was successful but frustrating. He led a skilful QPR side to within fifteen minutes of winning the League title, and he captained England before injury ended his international career when he was only twenty-four. In a brief stay at Crystal Palace, he teamed up with striker Mike Flanagan, who's pictured with another classic of its kind.

GERRY FRANCIS

KEVIN KEEGAN

1979 We're tempted to blame it on the perm. When he joined Liverpool, our Kev sported the close-cropped layers and sideburns of the time – and was an instant hit. As the hair got shaggier, success came just as thick and fast. His two goals won the 1974 FA Cup Final and he lifted the European Cup three years later, followed by a move to Hamburg and two European Footballer of the Year titles. But a sudden downturn coincided with the appearance of that full-blown perm. England bombed in the finals of Euro 1980, Hamburg lost the European Cup Final, and injury wrecked his chances in the 1982 World Cup finals. His stint as England manager was just as unhappy, but his successes at Newcastle, Fulham and Man City give him reason to wear the now grey hair with pride.

★
338

★
339

★
342

Ron Atkinson
& Remi Moses

1980	JAN	FEB	MAR	APL	MAY	JUN	JUL	AUG	SEP	OCT	NOV	DEC
1981	JAN	FEB	MAR	APL	MAY	JUN	JUL	AUG	SEP	OCT	NOV	DEC
1982	JAN	FEB	MAR	APL	MAY	JUN	JUL	AUG	SEP	OCT	NOV	DEC
1983	JAN	FEB	MAR	APL	MAY	JUN	JUL	AUG	SEP	OCT	NOV	DEC
1984	JAN	FEB	MAR	APL	MAY	JUN	JUL	AUG	SEP	OCT	NOV	DEC
1985	JAN	FEB	MAR	APL	MAY	JUN	JUL	AUG	SEP	OCT	NOV	DEC
1986	JAN	FEB	MAR	APL	MAY	JUN	JUL	AUG	SEP	OCT	NOV	DEC
1987	JAN	FEB	MAR	APL	MAY	JUN	JUL	AUG	SEP	OCT	NOV	DEC
1988	JAN	FEB	MAR	APL	MAY	JUN	JUL	AUG	SEP	OCT	NOV	DEC
1989	JAN	FEB	MAR	APL	MAY	JUN	JUL	AUG	SEP	OCT	NOV	DEC

1980–1989

Permanent Damage

This is when it all started to spiral out of control. An age of excess, when mullets roamed the earth and the tight perm refused to die out, when even alpha males like Bryan Robson and Peter Shilton were tempted off the straight and narrow. And there was nobody to tell Chris Waddle he didn't need two haircuts at the same time.

TOMMY CATON

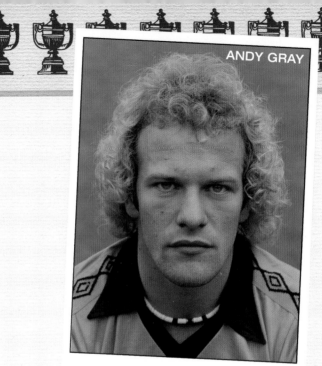

ANDY GRAY

1982 Two top players whose hairstyles often clashed on the pitch. Tommy Caton was an England prospect who sadly died young, a talented centre-half with Man City and Arsenal. Meanwhile, this is Andy Gray when he had hair and was every defender's nightmare: brave to the point of lunacy, always in your face. He scored in an FA Cup Final, a League Cup Final, and a Cup-Winners Cup Final.

Alan Biley

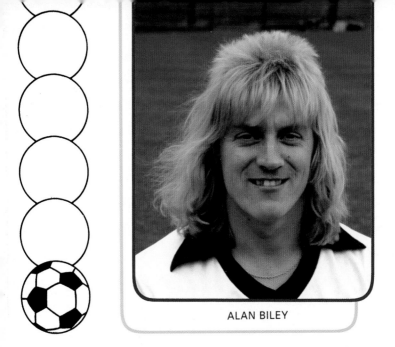

ALAN BILEY

1983 Alan was top goalscorer for Cambridge United when they won consecutive promotions, and for Portsmouth when they won the Third Division title – but do we really care? It's the barnet that matters here – and it's a real beauty. It looks like the love child of Mick Ronson (David Bowie's guitarist) and glam-rock band Sweet – but was probably all his own work. As you can see, it didn't change much with time – but then how do you improve on perfection? No more words now. Just gaze in awe.

1983

Alan Brazil was another bushy-haired striker who let it go on too long. Where were a footballer's advisors when he needed them? Alan Brazil was part of the talented Ipswich Town side who lifted the UEFA Cup in 1981 and should have won the League title at least once. He formed a dangerous partnership up front with Paul Mariner, whose style of play (and hair) complemented his. They were on opposite sides at Hampden Park in 1982, when Mariner scored the only goal of the game for England.

★
★
★
★
★
★

PAUL MARINER

NOEL BROTHERSTON

1984 When Noel Brotherston's Pre-Raphaelite bush began to wither, he couldn't bear to prune the rest of it. So we're faced with something like a clown's wig advancing towards us. But he had the last laugh in 1980, winning promotion with Blackburn Rovers and scoring the goal that gave Northern Ireland the Home Championship outright for the first time since 1914.

1985

We suspect 'Champagne' Charlie Nicholas began to believe his own publicity. Although he scored the goals that won a League Cup Final, his stint with Arsenal was better known for modelling assignments, publicity shots and his love of London's nightlife. The New Romantic mullet gave the critics some additional ammo. Shame, because the goal on his Scotland debut was a peach, flicking the ball from one foot to the other in mid-air before volleying in from long range.

TERRY CONNOR

152

GERRY GOW

153

GEOFF PALMER

GARY ARMSTRONG

LESLIE BARR

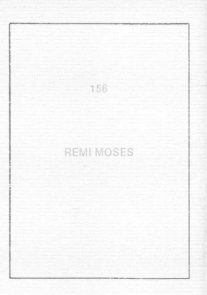

156

REMI MOSES

CRAIG JOHNSON

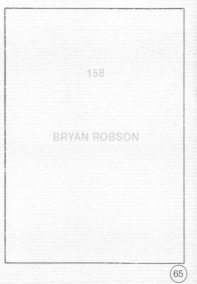

158

BRYAN ROBSON

Diamond Lights

1987 Hod & Wad were quite a double act. Their brilliance on the ball took Tottenham to an FA Cup Final, they both won more than 50 England caps despite being in and out of favour, and they even made the charts together. 'Diamond Lights', which reached No. 12 in 1987, wasn't that bad. They were known, rather prosaically, as Glenn & Chris on *Top of the Pops* when the name Hoddle & Waddle was crying out to be used.

Glenn
&
Chris

CHRIS WADDLE

1988 Chris & Glenn were equal partners – except when it came to hair. While 'Glennda' sported the typical Tottenham cut of the day, Waddle was unique. To us, he's still the boss. The Mullet King. He seemed to have endless permutations of short and spiky on top and long at the back.

Barry Venison

	JAN	FEB	MAR	APL	MAY	JUN	JUL	AUG	SEP	OCT	NOV	DEC
1990	JAN	FEB	MAR	APL	MAY	JUN	JUL	AUG	SEP	OCT	NOV	DEC
1991	JAN	FEB	MAR	APL	MAY	JUN	JUL	AUG	SEP	OCT	NOV	DEC
1992	JAN	FEB	MAR	APL	MAY	JUN	JUL	AUG	SEP	OCT	NOV	DEC
1993	JAN	FEB	MAR	APL	MAY	JUN	JUL	AUG	SEP	OCT	NOV	DEC
1994	JAN	FEB	MAR	APL	MAY	JUN	JUL	AUG	SEP	OCT	NOV	DEC
1995	JAN	FEB	MAR	APL	MAY	JUN	JUL	AUG	SEP	OCT	NOV	DEC
1996	JAN	FEB	MAR	APL	MAY	JUN	JUL	AUG	SEP	OCT	NOV	DEC
1997	JAN	FEB	MAR	APL	MAY	JUN	JUL	AUG	SEP	OCT	NOV	DEC
1998	JAN	FEB	MAR	APL	MAY	JUN	JUL	AUG	SEP	OCT	NOV	DEC
1999	JAN	FEB	MAR	APL	MAY	JUN	JUL	AUG	SEP	OCT	NOV	DEC
2000	JAN	FEB	MAR	APL	MAY	JUN	JUL	AUG	SEP	OCT	NOV	DEC

1990...

FIRST OF THE MOHICANS

Anything goes by now. When we celebrate the differences between us, uniform haircuts disappear. So has a lot of hair. There are more shaven heads than in the past – so you could say there's a uniform way of dealing with recession. But for everyone else the possibilities are endless.

So we've grown used to the sight of Christian Ziege trading his floppy fringe for a Mohican or a complete scalping. We're not stunned to see Henrik Larsson shave off his dreadlocks. And the head boy himself changes his mind almost as often as his club Man United replace their away strip. It just isn't a team game any more.

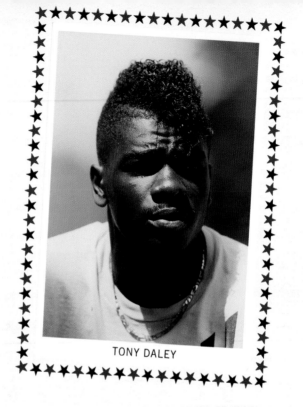

TONY DALEY

1994 Speedy Tony Daley generally kept it short at the sides but varied the area on top. Like his football, it wasn't quite in the Chris Waddle class, but he took the great man's place in the England team. His old Villa manager Graham Taylor picked him for the Euro finals in 1992, but he missed chances against the hosts Sweden, England lost and went out, and Daley wasn't capped again.

Once the TV comedians Baddiel and Skinner decided that Jason Lee's hairstyle looked like a pineapple, people couldn't take him seriously any more. The constant jibes got to him and he began missing chances. He scored only 14 goals in 76 League games for Forest and the pineapple became more of a fuzzy peach.

JASON LEE

1995 The little mascot in the picture probably dared to suggest that Vinnie Jones might try growing his hair for once. This is someone who made the most of what little he had. He carved out a career as an actor, a singer, and even as a footballer, winning the FA Cup with Wimbledon in 1988. If you're envious of all these strings he has to his bow, a least you can enjoy his international career. His first match for Wales ended in a 3-0 home defeat, he was sent off in another, and when he was made captain against Holland he told us 'You've got to get in amongst these good players.' Wales lost 7-1. Lock, stock and barrel.

Vinnie Jones

1996 Two icons of the Colombian game. There are no words to describe Valderrama's famous fashion statement, so we won't try. He was captain in almost all of his 111 internationals. After the last one, at the 1998 World Cup, he changed shirts with David Beckham. Passing on a mantle, plus the odd hairdressing tip no doubt. Last year a 33-foot statue of him was erected in his home town. We estimate thirty feet of him and three of the coiffure.

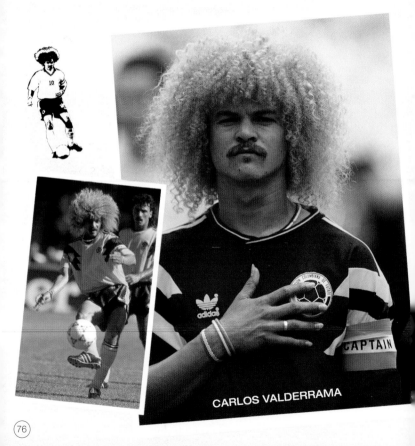

CARLOS VALDERRAMA

Higuita's scorpion kick against England at Wembley was typical of him. So was the way he lost the ball to Roger Milla while trying to dribble upfield, the ensuing goal knocking Colombia out of Italia '90. You get the picture: this was not your normal goalkeeper. He missed the 1994 World Cup after being jailed on kidnapping charges. Having scored from the penalty spot in three internationals, he spent the time inside practising free kicks.

RENÉ HIGUITA

1998 If you do this kind of thing to yourselves, you'd better win. After beating England in the 1998 World Cup, the whole Romanian team hit the peroxide (except the goalkeeper, who was bald). Chelsea's Dan Petrescu, who scored the winner against England, is third from the left. Romania struggled to draw with Tunisia then went out in the next round.

2002 Whichever way you look at it, these are six unmistakable players even without their names on their shirts. Roberto Baggio's 'divine ponytail' was a star of USA '94, but he'll probably be remembered for missing a penalty in the final. Cobi Jones played 159 times for the USA but only 25 for Coventry City. Hidetoshi Nakata and Clint Mathis scored in the last World Cup finals. We saw too much of Seaman's ponytail in endless re-runs of Ronaldinho's free kick. And Taribo West told us the green ribbons were here to stay 'because it's fun and it's fashionable'. So he was half right.

DAVID BECKHAM

2003 More than anyone else in the history of the game, David Beckham will be remembered as much for his hairstyle as for anything he managed on a football pitch. He's done it all – long and dyed, short and spiky, a £300 Number One – and even in an injury-hit World Cup 2002 he seemed to have started something. His old Mohican was now being used by Christian Ziege, Turkey's Umit Davala and Clint Mathis of the USA. If they start wearing sarongs, colouring their fingernails pink or trying on their celebrity wives' undies, we'll know where they got it from.

The Last Word in Haircuts

If what you've seen here has raised your eyebrows and dropped your jaw, be warned: the future holds more of the same. Ever since someone decided it was OK for men to care about their appearance, hair has grown in importance – and we can't see any reason for that to change.

www.footballershaircuts.co.uk

Reflections

Brian Little: *I had an allergy to barbers. It wasn't a conscious thing it just only got cut at the front when it went in my eyes and even then I did it myself. We were different to current players – we didn't care what we looked like. I use more hair gel now than I did then!* **PAGE 7**

Neil Warnock: *It was a great style I had – it saved me having to wash it!* **PAGE 34**

Charlie George: *Originally I had a skin head and decided to let it grow. The more people said get it cut, the more I grow it. After that I had a perm to be different but no-one remembers that or the skin head!* **PAGE 36**

Tony Currie: *A female journalist once wrote a newspaper article all about my hair – she called it the Thatched Barn look – I wasn't too pleased about that!* **PAGE 38**

Alan Brazil: *It was all natural you know not a perm. When you had hair like mine you can't do anything with it so I just had to let it go!* **PAGE 58**

Charlie Nicholas: *I asked for the Kevin Keegan cut but my hairdresser had been smoking funny fags that day!* **PAGE 62**

Barry Venison: *I was totally oblivious in those days to any kind of trends or fashion. I had the same haircut for about twelve years, just little changes in length and blondness (I wasn't a natural blonde you know!). I never changed it because I actually enjoyed the stick. It became part of my identity – that and the really dodgy clothes.* **PAGE 70**

Index

First published in the United Kingdom in 2003 by
Weidenfeld & Nicolson
Wellington House, 125 Strand
London, WC2R 0BB

Text copyright © Cris Freddi 2003

A CIP catalogue record for this book is available
from the British Library

ISBN 0-297-83090-2

Printed and bound in Italy

Created and edited by Matt Lowing
Designed by Emil Dacanay
Index by Mike Solomons

With special thanks to David Scripps, Stephen Guise and Graham Lowing.

The publishers would like to thank the following for permission to reproduce this
material. Every care has been taken to trace the copyright holders. However,
if there are any omissions we will happily rectify them in future editions.

With the exception of the following all photographs are courtesy of Action Images:

Colorsport: pages 2, 5, 7, 17, 22, 26
Hulton Getty: pages 6, 8, 37, 48, 80
(top left), 81 (top left), 82
Hutton Press: pages 10 (all images), 11
NFF Archive: page 12
Archiv Agon Sportverlag: page 13
Popperfoto: page 16 (right)